AF723771

# I Am Danny

By

Lori Bakewell

Based on the album by

V. B. Amster

Copyright © 2023 Lori Bakewell and Horse Tales
Song lyrics copyright © 2022 Valerie Banks Amster and Horse Tales

Print ISBN 979-8-218-29316-1
Ebook ISBN 979-8-218-29317-8

All rights reserved. No part of this publication may be reproduced, distributed, or transmitted in any form or by any means, including photocopying, recording, or other electronic or mechanical methods, without the prior written permission of the author or publisher, except in the case of brief quotations embedded in critical reviews and certain other noncommercial uses permitted by copyright law. For permission requests, contact Horse Tales at www.horsetales.org

First edition

Published by Horse Tales
Warrenton, Virginia, USA

# Contents

Chapter 1

# I Can **Love Myself**

A long time ago when I was a young colt, I realized something. I was not the same on the outside as all the other horses around me. Their **coats** were brown or sometimes black.

Mine was yellow. Yellow!

And oh, their faces were so handsome with dark fur and maybe a little white marking in just the right spot. Those faces looked perfect to me. Mine had a big **blaze.** I thought my white marking was too big!

**WHOA!**

Do you know what a horse's **coat** is? What about a **blaze**? A horse's coat is different from the coats we wear to keep warm. A horse's coat is the hair that covers its whole body! A blaze is a wide white marking between its eyes and sometimes down to its nose.

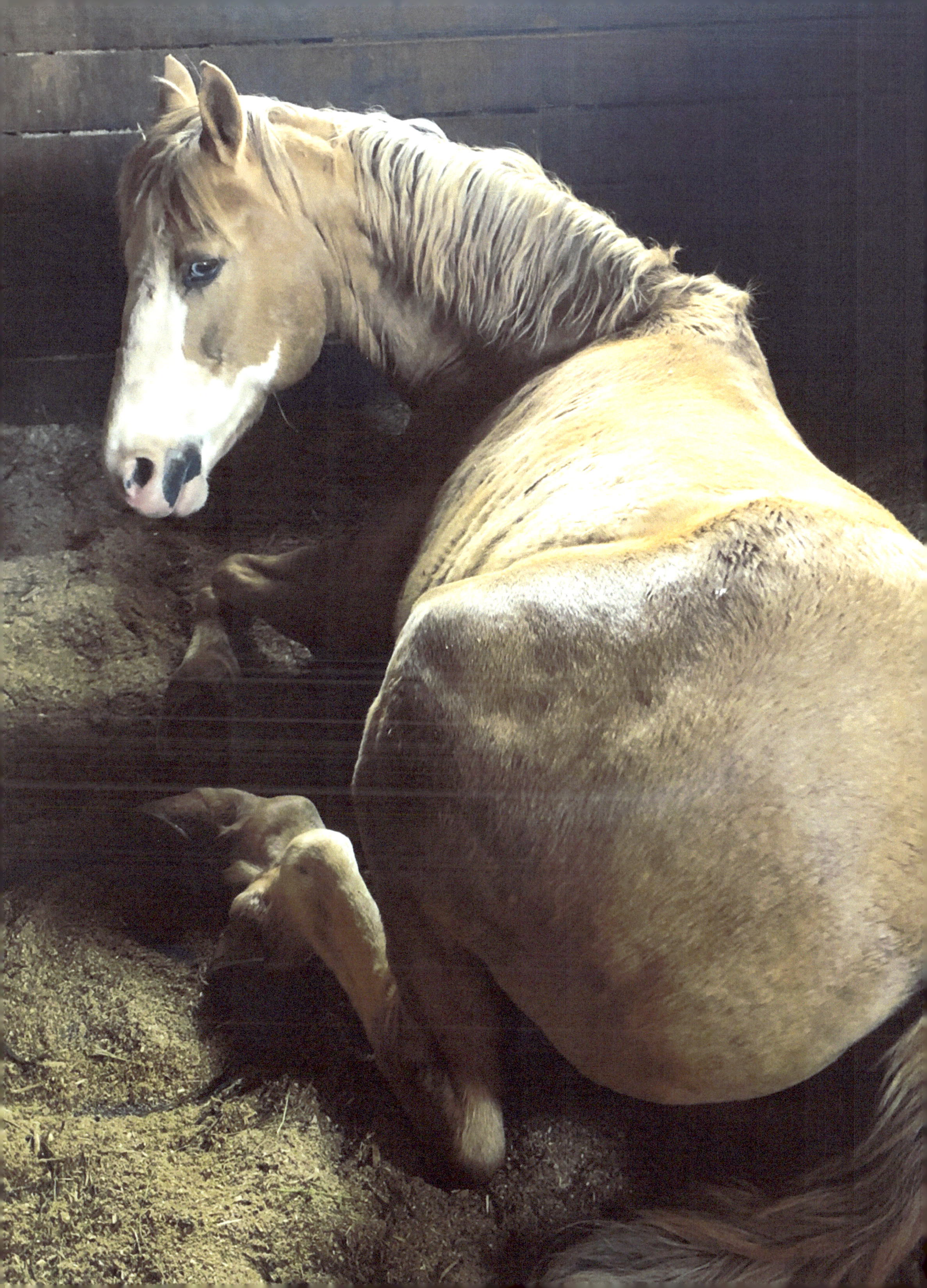

Why wasn't I like everyone else?

Yellow coat, white coat. I was so different. I even had blue eyes. But they weren't all blue. My left eye was a mixture of blue and brown. I didn't see eyes like that anywhere.

Every horse I saw looked different from me. I didn't want to be different. I wanted to be the same. Isn't it better if we are all exactly alike? That's what I thought. I didn't feel special. I didn't feel comfortable in my body with all its differences. It was hard to love myself because I didn't know who I was.

Why do I look so different from everyone else?

Then one day something wonderful happened. I met a human who thought I was perfect. She liked my coat. She liked my blaze. She liked my unusual eyes. And because I liked her, too, I started looking at myself differently.

I saw my strong body and all it could do…and then I loved my yellow and white coat because it was part of ME.

I saw love in my human's eyes when she looked at me…and then I loved my blue and brown eyes that could look back at her the same way.

How I looked and how the other horses looked was not so important anymore. What mattered was all I could do with my own wonderful fine self.

I could meet interesting people.

I could learn new things.

I could decide that being different was more than okay; it was perfect.

The outside of us comes in all kinds of sizes and shapes and colors. We're all different and that's the way we're supposed to be. When the inside of us, our hearts and spirits and minds, loves the outside, something amazing happens. We see how special we are and we see how special everyone else is, too.

Take it from me, Danny: Loving the world or even just one person all starts with loving yourself Once you do that, you can do anything.

## Danny says:

**You are beautiful and perfectly different inside and out and I am proud of you.**

**You can love yourself!**

Sing Along!

# A Horse of Many Colors

*All Sing Along song lyrics from the *I Am Danny* album by Horse Tales
Listen on Spotify, Apple Music, or any streaming service!

When I was just a colt, I could already see
The other horses all looked different from me
The fur on my front legs was a golden yellow
But it was brown and black on the other fellows

When I drank from the pond and I saw my face
A big white blaze curved all over the place
Other horses had a star or a stripe
But the fur on their faces was dark, not white

How can I be proud of my own fur
If all the other horses are a different color?
How do I know there are blue eyes around
When all the ones I see are chocolate brown?

The answers to these questions were hard to find
Until I met the human who would always be mine
She'd wanted a horse with golden fur
And my blue eyes made her soul stir

In the show ring all the judges would note
That I was the only paint palomino
My tall white stockings showed off my stride
My big blue eyes would open wide
My long white tail flew out behind me
And my golden coat gleamed as bright as could be

Maybe I'll be the only yellow horse
Who goes to a show to jump a course
But your coat doesn't matter, it matters what you do
Cause in the whole wide world, there's only one you

Chapter 2

# I Can **Lead**

Horse shows are fun but they are also a lot of work. I liked being a **paint palomino** and the way the judges noticed my colors. I liked practicing in the rings before competing and I really, **really** liked jumping.

Did I mention how much I liked jumping? That's right: I liked it a lot. **Really!**

These things were fun for me but I could not go to a show alone. I needed a partner. My human was the perfect partner for me.

**WHOA!**

Do you know what a **paint palomino** is? Danny had two different color traits. Being a palomino meant he had a golden coat with a white mane and tail. Being a paint meant that he had large white markings on his colored coat.

There was only one problem. I was strong and sure and comfortable but my human was not. She was nervous. We had worked very hard and I thought we were ready for state finals. My human did not really believe that. She was not quite ready to fly over the jumps with me.

The state finals did not go very well. Being a team meant we needed to trust each other. This is true for any team working together, whether they are horses or humans or one of each.

My human loved me and she knew what I could do, but the trust was not fully there. Her head knew but her heart was not ready and she pulled the reins tight. I couldn't fly over the jump.

Do you know anybody who is a little scared? Maybe they are nervous. Maybe they need time to learn to trust. What can you do to help them? How can you show them the way?

How can you be a leader?

I knew I needed to be the leader for my human. Leading means earning someone's trust by caring about them and guiding them.

After the **state finals** my human and I worked together a lot. I showed her that she could trust me and when she did, she also learned to trust herself as part of our team. Now we were able to fly over the jumps together.

The next time we went to state finals, we were a true team. Did we win a ribbon? No, not that time. I felt like a winner, though, because I found out what it means to be a leader.

You are a leader when you help someone learn and grow. You are a leader when you show them the way. If they trust you and you trust them, you both become stronger.

**Danny says:**

**You know how to be a friend and a helper. You can be trusted.**

**You can lead!**

**WHOA!**

The **state finals** are the last show of the year for horses and riders competing in a state horse show system. It's a multiday show that requires an overnight trip, so it's very exciting for riders who usually only compete at one-day horse shows!

# Fly with Me

We'd been showing quite a bit
Making it around the course
The human was still nervous
But I was a patient horse

So come one November
We went to the state finals
We schooled in both our rings
Getting ready for the trials

But when we went to jump
The human was so frightened
I did the best I could
As both my reins were tightened

Take a deep breath, human
You don't have to be so scared
We worked hard to get ready
I know how much you care

Let go and fly with me
I'll soar over every jump
Let go and fly with me
Cause flying's so much fun

The human was ashamed
Of the way she'd frozen up
So we got right back to work
And she learned to loosen up

She learned to canter with me
Instead of holding me back
We found our gait together
And we cruised around the track

And one year later
With ribbons under our belt
We got back in that ring
A new hand had been dealt

The human took a deep breath
And she didn't feel scared
She knew that she could trust me
I knew we were prepared

She let go and flew with me
We soared on a wing and a prayer
She let go and flew with me
She smiled in the air

I didn't win a ribbon
At the big state final show
But we did something bigger
That we would always know

And when she came to get me
For the trailer ride back home
I put my nose upon her chest
For a moment before we roamed

She looked into my eyes of blue
And she knew what we had done
It took a lot of faith and trust
But our hearts became one

The human learned to fly
She learned to trust my wings
Even when the stakes were high
We flew over everything

Let go and fly with me
I'll never let you down
Let go and fly with me
We soar through every round

## Neigh It Loud

One day there was a horse show away from the farm
The human thought going wouldn't do any harm
It was fun to have a new place to see
I rode over with the horses who live with me

The fences were little; we were just starting out
I jumped over all of them without any doubt
But the next time in the ring, what did I see?
A bunch of other horses were in there with me!

I felt so much excitement
It bubbled up inside
And before I knew it
I changed the whole ride

I let out a neigh!
I neighed long and loud
I let out a neigh!
I neighed for the crowd

The human was surprised and she tried
to distract me
But I loved when everyone turned to see
Which horse was making that magnificent sound
I took a deep breath, picked my hooves off the ground

I let out a neigh
I neighed long and loud
I let out a neigh
I neighed for the crowd

If you're ever surprised by the place that you're in
And feel so much excitement it pours out of your skin
Take a tip from me, and use your voice to say
How happy you are to be there that day

Let out a neigh
Neigh long and loud
Let out a neigh
Neigh for the crowd

Let's hear your neigh
Can you neigh long and loud?
Let's hear your neigh
Can you neigh with this crowd?

Chapter 3

# I Can **Follow**

I liked leading. Being the leader felt important to me. But after a while I started to notice that I was not always the leader. Sometimes someone else did the caring and the guiding.

I wasn't sure how I felt about that. After all, I was good at leading. If someone else did it, then I was the follower. I didn't know if I could be both.

**WHOA!**

Do you know what **stirrups** are? Stirrups are the metal objects that hang on both sides of the saddle for the rider's feet. They usually have a rubber surface on the bottom called a grip to help the rider's foot stay still in the stirrup.

Was I strong only when I was leading? That didn't seem right. I had to think about it for a while. I munched some hay and thought and thought and thought.

And munched and munched and thought some more.

Then it came to me. Hay! I was munching my hay, but guess what? I was not the one who brought the hay. The humans did that and a bunch of other things to take care of me.

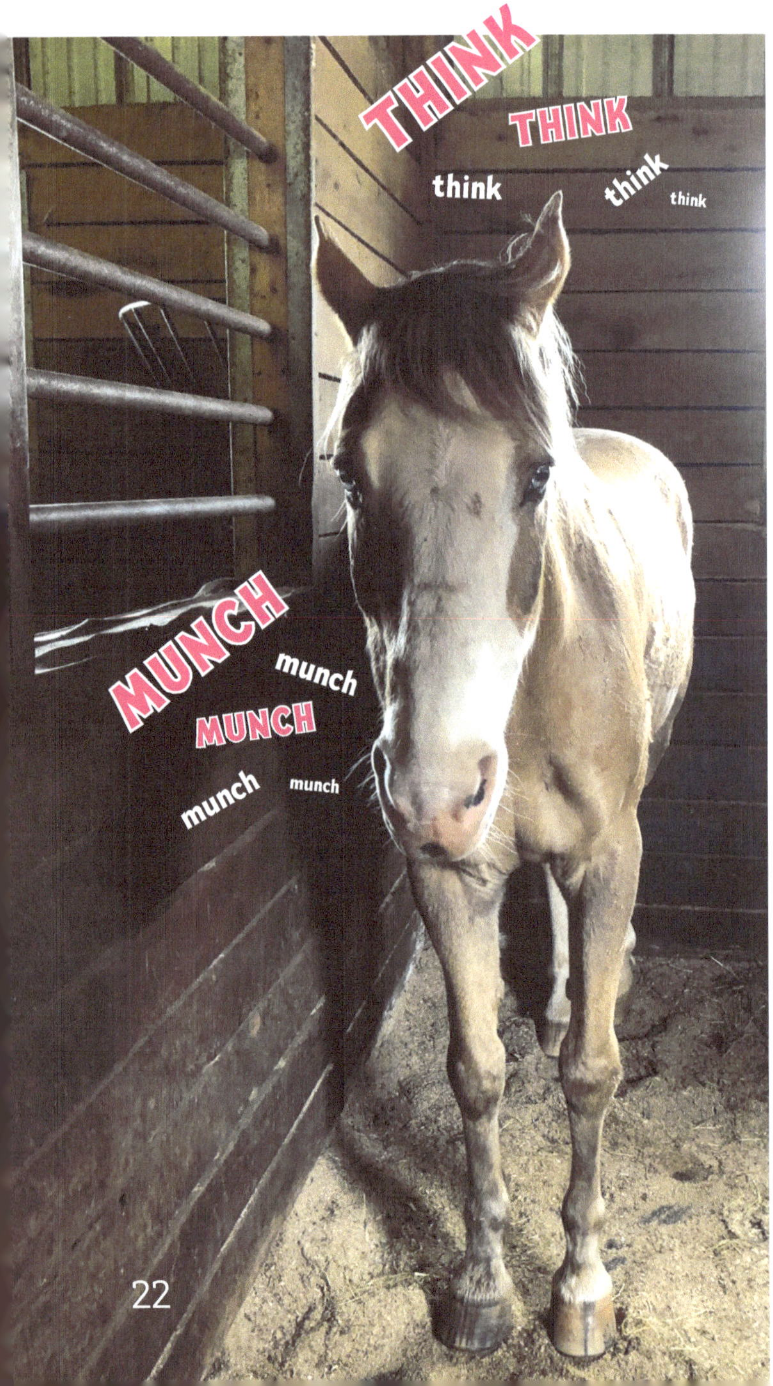

Horses need a herd, a group to keep them happy and safe. In the wild, there are leaders and followers in the herd and all the horses knows their places. It's different when a horse lives on a farm or in a barn. Sometimes the herd includes other animals, like goats.

Yes, goats. It's true.

And on a farm or in a barn the herd can include humans.

I depended on humans for all the good things I needed. They made sure I had food, water, shelter, and safety. I trusted my human to think about me and take care of me. I trusted her to be the leader I needed.

When she was the leader, what was I? Right! The follower.

WHOA!

Do you know what a horse uses a **rack** for? It is in the photo to the left, and Danny talks about his rack in the "Clean Stall" song. A hay rack holds the hay on the wall for a horse to munch on. Most horses need a LOT of hay or grass for forage. Humans toss a flake or two of hay into it to feed the horse.

Here's what I learned as I munched and thought: Leaders are strong, but so are followers. I could be either depending on where I was and who was with me and what we needed. Sometimes I was the helper and the guide. Sometimes I was the one being helped and guided. Both these roles needed trust and respect.

My human learned when to trust me to lead. She needed my strong legs and energy to carry us over a jump. I learned when to trust her to lead. I needed her to take care of me.

Leading is important and so is following. We all have something to teach and something to learn. When we put that together, when we help and trust each other, we are the strongest we can be.

## Danny says:

**Never be afraid to lead AND follow. You have so much to give to others and they have so much to give to you.**

**You can follow!**

## Itancan

The human read a book
By GaWaNi Pony Boy
About Lakota horsemanship
Techniques she could employ

Horse, Follow Closely
Was the title that she read
If she was my itancan
I'd follow where she led

The itancan's the herd leader
Horses go where they say
They keep us safe from danger
And always show the way

"I am your itancan"
She tells me at the gate
We go in the barn together
And she sets my saddle straight

My human's my itancan
I leave my herd when she calls
We become a herd of two then
She'll never let me fall

"I am your itancan"
As she leads me to the ring
She swings up in my stirrups
And I'd do anything

The itancan signals danger
When predators are near
If my itancan is relaxed
I have nothing to fear

My human's my itancan
I watch her like a hawk
Because our body language
Is the way that we can talk

My human's my itancan
I follow where she leads
On one step or a journey
I know just how to please

Sing Along!

# Clean Stall

I like a clean stall and I don't know why
Some horses live in a pig sty
They potty everywhere and spread their hay
all around
So there isn't any clean spot on the ground!

I like a clean stall so when I rest
The shavings feel like a soft, fresh nest
When I stretch out and put down my head
It's just like lying in your bed

Keeping things clean isn't hard to do
It just takes a little effort from you
Think about your space and how you want
it to be
And follow these tips that you learn from me

The humans work hard to keep things clean
I'm groomed every day til my coat gleams
My stall gets picked up every morning and night
So it never becomes a frightful sight

I love what they do so they'll never doubt
I'll do my part to help them out
A nice clean stall makes us all happy
And I don't get extra dirt on me

If my hay from the rack falls on the ground
I keep it all in a neat little mound
I choose another space when I have to go
There's no need for a mess, you know

Keeping things clean isn't hard to do
It just takes a little effort from you
Think about your space and how
you want it to be
And follow these tips that you learn
from me

Chapter 4

# I Can Be Grateful

We all have so many choices every day. Do we use kind words or do we sound impatient? Do we learn from our mistakes or act like they don't matter? Do we try new things or hang on to what we know?

Do we eat our alfalfa first or our other hay?

Life is full of experiences. Sometimes things don't work out the way you think they will. Maybe things get better. Maybe things don't seem better at all.

**WHOA!**

I bet you know what hay is, but do you know what **alfalfa** is? Alfalfa is a kind of hay, and it is usually the highest in protein, calories, and calcium. When it is part of a horse's diet, it is usually balanced with hays like timothy, orchard grass, and brome.

Do you want to know one thing I found out? Life, with all its choices and all its experiences, is an adventure. I enjoyed exploring that adventure and along the way I learned a lot and laughed a lot and loved a lot. Every day has something worth exploring, don't you think?

When my human was hurt after I bucked at an evening show, I knew I had made a bad choice. That was not a happy experience, but I learned from my mistake. When she was better we tried something new at horse shows and we found out that being a **pleasure horse team** was exactly right for both of us.

Every day when I finished working and playing, I got to rest in a beautiful clean stall or out in a field with the other horses. There was always something or someone to watch. Did that make me happy? You know it!

When I felt happy, everybody knew it. My eyes lit up. I went right to my human and rubbed my face on her. Sometimes I even let out a **nicker**!

WHOA!

Do you know what a **pleasure horse team** is? In a pleasure horse division, the horse is judged on how well it moves, and how fun it looks to ride. The human tries to show off the horse and make it look like it is very easy to ride for a long time.

Do you know what **nicker** is? A nicker is a happy noise that a horse makes when he is excited about something.

Gratitude means being thankful. I think noticing little things that make us happy can grow into an attitude of gratitude. You can even make a list! I'll share mine.

## Danny's attitude of gratitude list:

1. 
Shade from a tall tree that feels so good on a hot day

2. 
Friends who come in all sizes and shapes and colors

3. 
A kind voice telling me that I am loved

4. 
The breeze that ruffles my mane at a horse show

5. 
A pile of yummy hay

6. 
Riding with my human

7. 
Helping small humans learn what it's like to sit on a broad back way up high

8. 
A new adventure waiting for me on the other side of the trailer door

Every one of those things was new the first time I experienced it. Was everything perfect all the time? No. But it seems like there was always something I could look at and appreciate. Maybe it was a very small something and I had to look very hard to find it. When I did, I learned that noticing a very small something is one way to make it seem bigger and more important.

## Danny says:

**Look all around you. What makes your heart happy? That's gratitude! Add up all those good things and before you know it you might have to laugh out loud. Or even neigh!**

**You can be grateful.**

# A Hidden Champion

One night at an evening show
The air was cool, the sky aglow
I felt so happy after a jump
I put down my head and tossed up my rump

I was just feeling playful, but the next thing I knew
Into the air the human flew
Her muscle was torn; someone put me away
She went home to ride another day

The human got hurt because I threw a buck
I was rather horror struck

That day came soon, but it would be a while
Before we could jump in our usual style
So we entered a class judged on how I went
This turned out to be money very well spent

The human rode lightly, with barely a touch
I turned on a dime and halted and such
When the results were announced loud and clear
I won my first blue ribbon of the year

Could we make something good come from
that buck
Or was that show beginners luck?

Class after class, night after night
The pleasure horse division was our delight
I was handy, I was smooth, and I didn't bat an eye
If another naughty horse went bucking by

We tried something new and uncovered our skill
Now our journey wasn't so uphill

We used my mistake to open up a new world
And the champion in me started to unfurl
We were top in the show, the region, the state
We were the ones to beat, no matter the slate

Thanks to what we did after that impulsive buck
I'll always be a champion, and that's not luck

Sing Along!

## Let's Explore

When I was an old horse of 22
The human said, "I have a new barn for you.
The people there will give you the best of care
And you'll have lots of clean, fresh air."

The trailer came and I walked right in
A new adventure was about to begin
Marshall the warmblood needed a friend
A calm, steady horse on which to depend

You're never too old to see new places
Don't have to be shy when you meet new faces
There are always new things to explore
On the other side of the trailer door

In the next months, there was so much to see
We walked in the woods, my human and me
We rode down the driveway and in every field
I nudged every gate to see which ones would yield

I sipped from every bucket and grazed on all the grass
I put my head out so people pet me as they passed
Marshall and I frolicked and stood in the shade
That the tall leafy trees of the forest made

You're never too old to see new places
Don't have to be shy when you meet new faces
There are always new things to explore
On the other side of the trailer door

They took such good care of me, with alfalfa at midday
And a manger on my wall that was always full of hay
The minis were groomed outside my stall
This adventure was the best—I was grateful for it all

You're never too old to see new places
Don't have to be shy when you meet new faces
There are always new things to explore
On the other side of the trailer door

Chapter 5

# King Danny

Everything changes, my friends. Look around and you'll see what I mean. The sky changes from the glow of dawn to the deep darkness of night. That happens every day. Isn't that amazing? And what about the trees? The ones that drop their leaves and look so bare end up full and beautiful again in the spring. Have you ever planted a flower seed and watched it grow and make a seed pod of its own and return the next year, prettier than ever? So much beautiful change!

**WHOA!**

Do you know what **dressage** is? It is mentioned on page 42. In dressage, the horse and rider compete in a rectangular ring with a very low fence. The rider memorizes a test, or series of movements, and the horse and rider are scored on how well they perform them.

You're growing and changing, too. Maybe your clothes no longer fit. Maybe you go to a new school where you are learning new things and making new friends. Sometimes things you once liked don't fit in your life now. Just as your body grows and your mind grows, your emotions grow and change, too.

Remember how I didn't like the way I looked? I was different from the other horses and all I wanted was to be the same. My looks never changed but my heart did. Who needs to be like everyone else? Not me!

I was not always a calm, happy horse. It's true! There were times when I was not a leader and I was not a follower and I did not know how to be part of a team.

But guess what? I changed. Just as I learned to love my looks, I also learned to love myself.

I was king of my world!

**A king guards and guides everyone around him.** When I watched over my friends and my humans, I felt good and strong. I loved that feeling.

**A king sets an example.** I knew what it was like to feel left out so I made sure every new horse had a friend right away. That friend was me!

**A king stays calm.** Fussing and fighting did not help me or the other horses. When I watched and waited, I found out a lot more.

**A king lets someone else take the lead and teach.** I did not know everything. When I trusted my teachers, I learned so much. I loved that feeling, too.

**A king is thankful.** I looked at all the beautiful things around me and I felt grateful for what I had and the big wonderful life I lived. I loved that feeling most of all.

## Danny says:

**Every day is new. Every day is a chance for you to be exactly who you're meant to be. Start by loving yourself: how you look, everything you can do, everything you can learn. When I did that, I became the best ME!**

**You can be the best YOU!**

Sing Along!

## King Danny

When I first came to my barn
I was a scrappy little thing
I picked fights with other horses
Tried to prove something

When they led me to my stall
I bolted for my feed
Once I broke the ribs
Of the person with my lead

But as I grew older
And stayed longer in my field
Something started changing
I became more even keeled

I became King Danny
I was the head of state
I guided the young geldings
They moved for me at the gate

A king protects his subjects
And considers what they need
I looked at my friends
And they asked me to lead

A king sets an example
And includes everyone
So when new horses would join us
I made sure that this was done

A king lets others take charge
I'd give a ride to anyone
A king has a sense of humor
We always had such fun

I became King Danny
I stayed calm and cool
Even when the others fought
I kept a steady rule

When you remember me
Think of how I led
Think of how I listened
Think of what I said

Think of the lessons I taught
How I was loyal and true
Remember how I was me
I always want you to be you

Sing Along!

# Cat on the Track

As I grew older, it was hard to keep jumping
So the human thought that we could try
a new thing
We landed on dressage, and we studied
patterns new
I learned to halt square and still for a beat
or two

We went to a show at a barn that was nearby
They had friendly, pretty cats that really caught
my eye
One climbed in the human's car and sunbathed
on the dash
As we went into the ring to show, another dashed
right past!

We made our salute and I trotted off brightly
Turned to the left and did a circle at E
Came across the diagonal and headed for
the back
And all of a sudden, the cat jumped on
the track!

There's a cat on the track!
What do we do?
There's a cat on the track
And he's looking at you!

We looked at each other and neither one
would budge
I went trotting on and the human asked
the judge,
"There's a cat on the track! What do I do?"
The judge said, "Come off the track and
carry through."

I yielded off the wall and I picked up my canter
The human smiled like a happy camper
Our score that day was the best we ever got
Cause the human asked the question and I kept
my bright trot

There was a cat on the track!
What did we do?
There was a cat on the track
So we asked someone who knew

If there's a cat on your track
And you don't know what to do
Find someone with the facts
And ask how to get through

# ★ Future Stars ★

Would you like to meet some of the stars of future Horse Tales books?
I would like to proudly introduce you to:

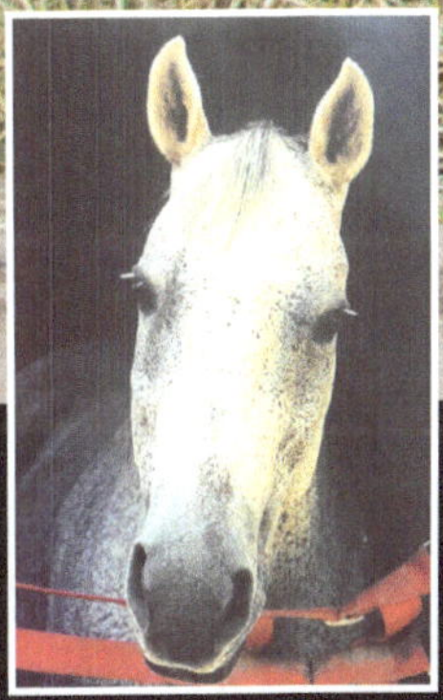
Boo

Feather

Sember

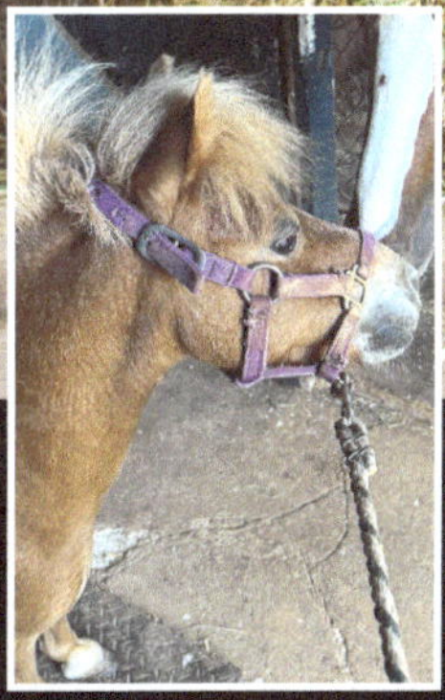
Mimi

Johnny

Nan the Mule

# Acknowledgements

## Danny's human sends loud neighs of gratitude to...

....**her Papa Joe** for unknowingly financing the purchase of her second horse, and sharing her lifelong love for the animals.

...**her husband Mike** and friend Stephanie for creating barn time for her.

...**Kristy Willwerth and Picturesque Farm** for taking Danny (then called Mario) in on sales consignment, facilitating his purchase, and training him and his human through all their triumphs and shenanigans.

...**Christie, Rigo, and Wilmar** for Danny's daily care for over a decade.

...**Dr. Steve White** and the doctors at Piedmont Equine Practice for Danny's veterinary and dental care.

...**Roxanne Haddon, Susie and Gita Grady, Kelsey and Scott McDowell, Jules Ianuzzi** and **Amanda Mills, Carmen and Traci Cantrell, Caroline Taylor, Sister Mary Bernard** and **Shawn Teer, Julie Nagel,** and **the Toal, Hailey, Reed, and Stremple families** for making riding and showing together so much fun.

...**Jen Cook** for our foray into dressage, and training us to surprisingly good scores for our first shows. Also **Jen, Linda Sautter,** and **Marina Frano** for teaching the human's children so they could enjoy riding and showing together.

....**The Picturesque Farm summer campers,** the children of our friends, the short stirrup riders who showed Danny, and the many teenagers and young adults who jumped on after he bucked his human off to sort things out.

...**Jordan and Grace Koepke and Sligo Stables** for giving him the most welcoming home for the end of his life, and appreciating him for the unique gelding that he was.

...**the songwriters in The Overcoats online class** and the **Children's Music Network song critique group** for helping me edit and clarify my messages in this album.

...**Elena Tal** for working through demo versions of the songs with me, tuning pitches and adjusting chords.

...**Mo Safren** for getting my vision for the album and running with it, making these songs even bigger and better than I could have imagined.

...**Craig Dye** for his trumpet and **Tanner Carlton** for all of his skills in bringing the album to fruition.

...**Lori Bakewell and her family** for knowing and loving Danny, and bringing him to life in words as only she can.

...**all of our photographer friends** for capturing his spirit and our journey in photos along the way.

...**Jennifer Anderson** for her meticulous design and creative touches in bringing yet another Horse Tales book to life on the page.

---

# Image credits

**Anna Purdy** cover photo, 10, 17, 25, 33, 37, 38, 40
**Valerie Banks Amster** pages 5, 7, 9, 11, 19, 21, 22, 23, 30, 31, 32, 43
**Jordan Koepke** pages 6, 15, 29, 32, 43
**Alyssa Amster** pages 23, 32
**Amanda Lynch Mills** pages 8, 13, 14, 16, 24, 32
**Jennifer Buffalo** page 9
**David Bell** page 16
**Margreta Grady** page 31
**Carrie Reed** page 32
**Mary Cornish-Hicks** page 38
**Roxanne Haddon** page 39
**Mary Catherine Anderson** page 38
**Illustrations: Adobe Stock/Jennifer Anderson** pages 11, 18,19, 26,27, 32, 34, 35 , 41, 42

www.ingramcontent.com/pod-product-compliance
Ingram Content Group UK Ltd.
Pitfield, Milton Keynes, MK11 3LW, UK
UKHW061032310726
14089UKWH00009B/208
* 9 7 9 8 2 1 8 2 9 3 1 6 1 *